DISCOVER
Sir Isaac Newton

by Barbara Brannon

Table of Contents

Introduction		2
Chapter 1	What Did Sir Isaac Newton Study?	4
Chapter 2	What Did Newton Learn About Motion?	10
Chapter 3	Why Is Newton Important?	14
Conclusion		18
Concept Map		20
Glossary		22
Index		24

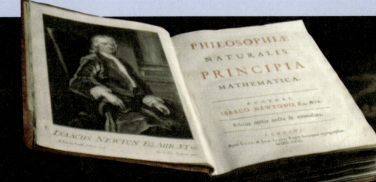

Introduction

Sir Isaac Newton was a **scientist**. Sir Isaac Newton was important.

▲ Sir Isaac Newton

Words to Know

 direction

 forces

 gravity

 motion

 scientist

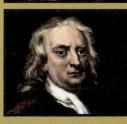 Sir Isaac Newton

See the Glossary on page 22.

Chapter 1

What Did Sir Isaac Newton Study?

Newton studied science.

▲ Sir Isaac Newton learned about science.

Newton studied math.

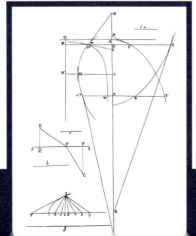

◄ Sir Isaac Newton learned about math.

Newton studied **gravity**.

▲ Sir Isaac Newton learned about gravity.

It's a Fact
Newton was the first to study gravity.

Chapter 1

Newton studied **motion**.

▲ Sir Isaac Newton learned about motion.

What Did Sir Isaac Newton Study?

Newton studied the sky.

▲ Sir Isaac Newton learned about the sky.

Newton studied planets.

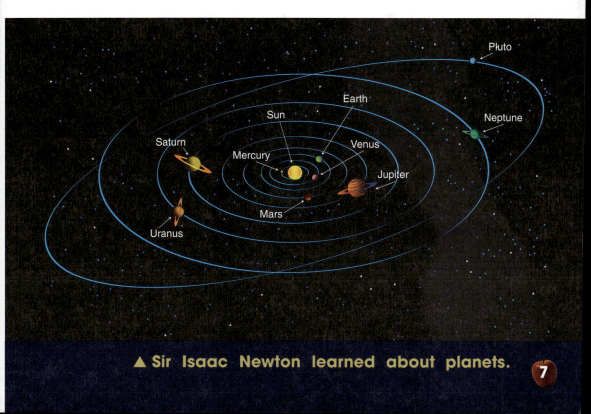

▲ Sir Isaac Newton learned about planets.

Chapter 1

Newton studied light.

▲ Sir Isaac Newton learned about light.

What Did Sir Isaac Newton Study?

Newton studied color.

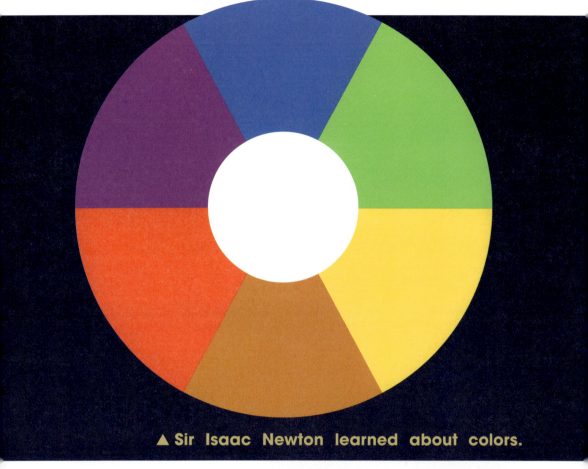

▲ Sir Isaac Newton learned about colors.

It's a Fact

Newton studied rainbows. Newton learned about rainbows. Newton said rainbows were drops of water.

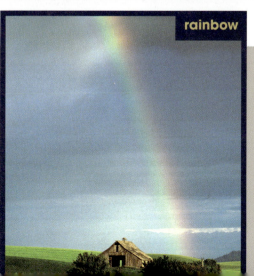

rainbow

Chapter 2

What Did Newton Learn About Motion?

Newton learned what causes motion.

▲ The football is in motion.

It's a Fact

Newton learned about motion. Some things push objects. Some things pull objects.

▲ The water pushes the boat.

▲ The tow truck pulls the car.

Chapter 2

Newton learned how objects change **direction**.

▲ The ball changes direction.

What Did Newton Learn About Motion?

Newton learned how **forces** work in pairs.

▲ The balloon is in motion. Gases from the balloon are in motion.

Chapter 3

Why Is Newton Important?

Newton learned about motion.

▲ Newton studied the forces of motion.

Newton was an inventor. Newton made the first cat door. The cat pushes the door. The door is in motion.

Newton learned about gravity.

▲ Newton studied the force of gravity.

Chapter 3

Newton learned about stars.

Did You Know?

Newton was an inventor. Newton made a new type of telescope.

▲ Newton studied the stars.

Why Is Newton Important?

Newton learned about planets.

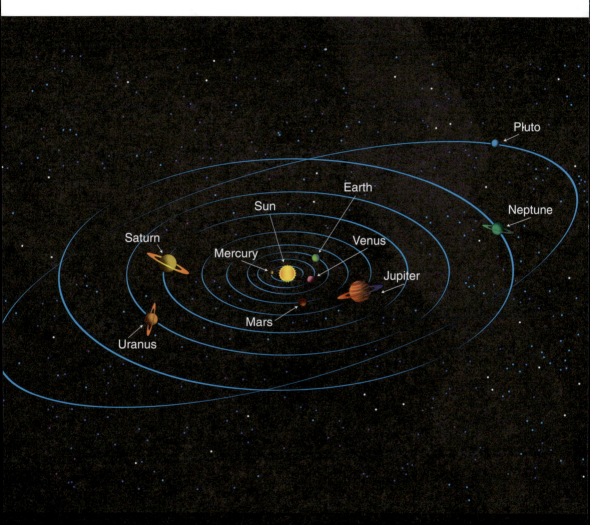

▲ **Newton studied the motion of planets.**

Conclusion

Newton was a scientist. Newton was a very important scientist.

Concept Map

Sir Isaac Newton

What Did Sir Isaac Newton Study?
- science
- math
- gravity
- motion
- sky
- light
- color

What Did Newton Learn About Motion?
- what causes motion
- how objects change direction
- how forces work in pairs

Why Is Newton Important?

studied motion

studied gravity

studied stars

studied planets

Glossary

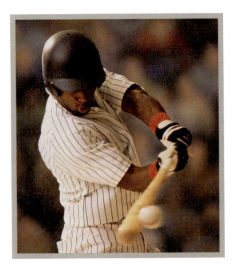

direction the way an object moves

*Newton learned how objects change **direction**.*

forces powers that make an object move

*Newton learned how **forces** work together.*

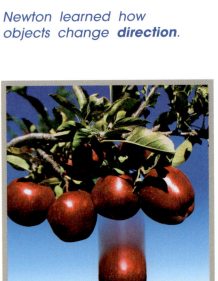

gravity a natural force

*Newton studied **gravity**.*

motion the act of moving

*Newton learned about **motion**.*

scientist a person who studies science

*Newton was a **scientist**.*

Sir Isaac Newton a scientist who studied motion

***Sir Isaac Newton** was a very important scientist.*

Index

color, 9, 20

direction, 12, 20

forces, 13–15, 20

gravity, 5, 15, 20–21

light, 8, 20

math, 4, 20

motion, 6, 10–11, 13–14, 17, 20–21

objects, 11–12, 20

Newton, Sir Isaac, 2, 4–18, 20–21

planets, 7, 17, 21

science, 4, 20

scientist, 2, 18

sky, 7, 20

stars, 16, 21